A HAPPY SPACE

Protect and Cherish
Your Bodies and Minds

BY IRASTINE PRESTON

Inspired Forever Book Publishing
Dallas, Texas

A Happy Space: Protect and Cherish Your Bodies and Minds

Copyright © 2019 Irastine Preston

All rights reserved, including the right of reproduction in whole or in part in any form without prior written permission, except in the case of brief quotations embodied in critical reviews and certain other noncommercial uses permitted by copyright law.

Inspired Forever Book Publishing™
"Words with Lasting Impact"
Dallas, Texas
(214) 444-6062
https://www.inspiredforeverbooks.com

Printed in the United States of America
Library of Congress Control Number: 2019911546

Paperback ISBN-13: 978-1-948903-23-3

Disclaimer: Any resemblance to actual persons, living or dead, or actual events is purely coincidental.

TABLE OF CONTENTS

PROTECT AND CHERISH YOUR MINDS..3

PROTECT AND CHERISH YOUR SELF-RESPECT..................................7

PROTECT AND CHERISH YOUR INDEPENDENCE............................11

PROTECT AND CHERISH YOUR IDEALS...15

PROTECT AND CHERISH YOUR VALUES...17

PROTECT AND CHERISH YOUR FAITH..21

PROTECT AND CHERISH YOUR PERSONAL SPACE........................25

ABOUT THE AUTHOR..49

INTRODUCTION

I loved school and never wanted to miss a day. As a woman, with the freedom to think for myself, I enjoyed learning new things like how to fix my hair, match clothes, and of course drive. Getting my license taught me the meaning of freedom; it opened my mind to many possibilities ahead. But, while I had an instructor to teach me how to drive, no one ever taught me that men could take up my personal space. I had to learn for myself that the wrong relationship could lead to having my thoughts and needs put last, or disregarded altogether—as if I didn't deserve any consideration as a person.

For me, just dating was not enough, so I decided to get married. This seemed like the right path for me, and for a year I was on Cloud Nine. Then, in what seemed like an instant I was pregnant, and that's when everything changed in a way I never expected. My life became about staying home with the babies all day long. Granted, I love my babes, but I never imagined that life would be all about cooking, cleaning *and* taking care of my husband. Suddenly I was expected to do everything at his bidding. This left no time for me or the things I needed. To fall in love is one thing, but to be valued less, or differently, after marriage was a disappointment.

PROTECT AND CHERISH
YOUR MINDS YOUNG LADIES

As a young, single person, your thoughts and feelings belong to you, but when you get married or have children that can change quickly. Suddenly, you may find there's no or space for yourself. All your thoughts become focused elsewhere. Just when you put the baby down to sleep, your duties can start all over with cooking, cleaning, and washing clothes. If you're thinking about marriage, you need to spend some time thinking about how you can protect your space. You can do that by remembering that your space belongs to you.

It's especially hard to protect your space if you start having children at an early age, in your teens for example. At that age, you'll be giving up your own youth for your children. Even if you marry between twenty and thirty years of age, there is so much of life that you could miss.

Learn to savor your single life. Get a job. Save your money. Take a trip, and not to your mom or dad's house where you'll be sleeping on the couch.

EMPOWERING THOUGHT:

Learn to appreciate the things that make you happy, or they may disappear.

PROTECT AND CHERISH
YOUR SELF-RESPECT YOUNG LADIES

When it comes to choosing a man, be sure you look for more than good looks. Choose someone responsible with an active mind who is interested in your thoughts and feelings and can work in partnership with you to complete daily tasks and monthly expenses. If sex is all he sees you for, get rid of him fast. Otherwise, you're apt to find yourself pregnant and your space will be taken up with doctor appointments for nine months and side effects like morning sickness and physical discomforts that come from carrying a child. Then comes the baby, the romantic hugs and kisses have disappeared, and you don't have the space you once had, or the good looking athletic man that seemed to have everything you wanted.

He has gone on with is life. Now you have found out he has someone else and suddenly he cares the most about her; she is now getting the hugs and kisses and you are at home with the baby. You're taking the baby to the doctor's appointment alone while he's with someone else. Then the inevitable happens and he comes back home. But by then he has dropped out of college and made two other women pregnant. All this just because you wanted a good-looking man instead of looking for a kind and supportive romantic partner.

EMPOWERING THOUGHT:

When you're choosing a man, look for something other than good looks. Be sure he has the qualities you want.

PROTECT AND CHERISH
YOUR INDEPENDENCE YOUNG LADIES

So you made the mistake of choosing a man for all the wrong reasons. How are you going to ensure you find your own space again and go on to build your own life? What are you going to do when he comes to you again, and tries to sweet-talk himself into your space once again?

Think about what you risk in giving up your space again. This man has betrayed you and actually made two other women pregnant. Are you willing to give up your space again, when he has no job, no place to live, and has dropped out of college? Consider keeping your own space instead of giving it away to someone who does not deserve you.

EMPOWERING THOUGHT:

Before you give up your space for a man,
look at what you'll be giving up.

PROTECT AND CHERISH
YOUR IDEALS YOUNG LADIES

Imagine this scenario: Your first baby is now eight years old, and going to school. Now you have your space back somewhat, you pick that baby up from school, you cook, clean, wash clothes. Will you give up your space for Mr. Good Time? While it may be hard to face reality, the truth is that he just needs a way out of his parents' house. They are giving him the blues because he realizes they expect him to take care of his own responsibilities and now he sees you doing well. So, he tells you he loves you and you start to feel those old feelings again. But do the right thing: Hold onto your ideals and keep your space for yourself, and for your child who deserves to be valued as well.

EMPOWERING THOUGHT:

Your ideals are what make you special,
so be sure you hold onto them.

PROTECT AND CHERISH
YOUR VALUES YOUNG LADIES

Just when you get the other mess out of your life, there is always someone else you start to fall for next. You fall for him at work, meeting him in the break room. But then you start to see that, like the man in your past, this man lacks values.

Will you let go of the space you have worked so hard to hold now?

Notice that I am asking you the same question over and over again - to get your attention. This book is about how certain men tend to take up space, leaving you with no time for yourself. If you give up the space for the wrong man, there will be no more getting hair and nails done, no more time to spend with your friends, no more mall shopping or spending money, no more time to relax and do what you like best. You'll just have endless chores, and bills, and appointments for the baby. Are you willing to give that space up for him? Take a long look at the space you are missing, and see that men are the reason you have lost the space in your life. You may be missing that space every day, and feel the weight of a life without any for your own. Believe me, that can make for a long, hard life. You owe it to yourselves to take a minute to consider how you might have a better life.

EMPOWERING THOUGHT:

Remember that the wrong man will only take over your space without adding anything value to your relationship.

PROTECT AND CHERISH
YOUR FAITH YOUNG LADIES

The time comes when you're sure you have found the right man and feel it's time to take a risk again. Before you take the leap, take a look at where you are now; look at all that you have accomplished in your life. You have raised a child, you now have a good job and your space back. Hold onto all that God has done for you. Once your child is older, send him or her off to college, keep your job, hold your head up; don't look down at the old things in your past. Keep moving up.

Perhaps a day will come when you will get married again. But before you do, take the proper safeguards. Please check him out. Don't only consider how good he looks, or if he has a nice body. Pick up the phone, do a background check and learn as much as you can about his past. Does he have a criminal record, bad credit, a bad temper, or health issues? Meet his family and learn all you can about how he was raised and how he treats his parents and siblings. Protect your space from someone who could literally destroy your life. This is not too much to ask for yourself!

EMPOWERING THOUGHT:

Don't commit yourself to someone until you do a background check, and never let go of your own space.

PROTECT AND CHERISH
YOUR PERSONAL SPACE YOUNG LADIES

You see, I allowed my space to be taken away because I was in love; my space was taken by the man that I thought loved me and only me. But that love went away. I cleaned house, cooked the meals, tended to the kids, and washed the clothes, but that was not good enough for him. Even though I had his three beautiful babies, I was not enough for him. In the end, the only time we spent together was between the sheets. Although we were married, the love was gone. He put someone else in his space, so I divorced him once my babies were grown.

Six years later, it started all over with another man. Although I saw in him the same things as in the last man, I fell in love and life was all warm and fuzzy.

Eventually, I thought about my own space, especially when he began to tell me that he was in love with another woman at this job and how he could not get other women off his mind. So you might think I would have left him immediately, but I thought if I prayed for him that lust for other women would disappear.

To this day, I am still working to understand my man's lust. God forgave me of my sins, so after fifteen years, I tried to give him some more time. Luckily, I hadn't given up my space and was keeping my eyes open.

EMPOWERING THOUGHT:

Don't give up your space
and keep your eyes open.

GOD GAVE ME A CHANCE

Just when is it time for all of us to take our space back? Will you and God have a talk so you can ask him to forgive you for your sins? Check yourself first, step back and see if you have been the reason your space was taken. Ask why you would allow someone to do this to you.

When you face yourself you can stand up to anything and everything. I checked myself and I found something wrong. I thought I could fix the man in my life, but as time went on I learned that I could not. So I gave him to God and asked God to work on both of us, but as God worked on us, my man continued to do the same - and no better. So I asked God how long this would continue to go on. And then I heard a sweet voice say, "No more."

You see, no matter how much you do, if that man still tells you how nice the next young lady looks, the relationship is in trouble. If he is with you and can't keep his mind on what's going on in real life, or if you are with him in a mall or some other place and his eyes are all over the place looking at other women, that tells you that this young man is not for you.

When his time is up, don't rush out to find another replacement. Think about your space. Otherwise, your new man may be no better and your space will be lost again!

EMPOWERING THOUGHT:

Let God help you regain your space.

Enjoy Your Life. Keep your space in the name of Jesus. Amen.

PROTECT AND CHERISH
ALL THINGS SACRED TO YOU....

PROTECT AND CHERISH YOUR SINGLE YEARS.

LEARN TO ENJOY BEING SINGLE AND DON'T RUSH INTO MARRIAGE BEFORE YOU'RE READY.

PROTECT AND CHERISH YOUR OWN INTERESTS.

CULTIVATE YOUR OWN INTERESTS BEFORE YOU DEDICATE YOUR LIFE TO MARRIAGE AND FAMILY.

PROTECT AND CHERISH YOUR SELF-RESPECT.

DON'T COMMIT YOURSELF TO
SOMEONE WHO
DOESN'T RESPECT YOU.
THAT'S A RECIPE FOR DISASTER.

PROTECT AND CHERISH TIME FOR YOURSELF.

BE SURE TO CARVE OUT TIME IN YOUR LIFE FOR YOURSELF. THAT'S HOW YOU'LL SAFEGUARD YOUR OWN SPACE.

PROTECT AND CHERISH YOUR RIGHT TO BE LOVED FOR WHO YOU ARE.

PROTECT AND CHERISH
YOUR IDEALS.

IT'S YOUR COMMITMENT TO IDEALS
IN LIFE THAT MAKE YOU
WHO YOU ARE.

PROTECT AND CHERISH YOUR VALUE SYSTEM.

THIS WILL KEEP YOU ON THE RIGHT PATH TO HOLDING YOUR OWN SPACE.

PROTECT AND CHERISH
YOUR FAITH IN GOD.

IT'S GOD'S LOVE THAT WILL LEAD YOU TO YOUR SACRED SPACE.

About the Author

Irastine Preston wrote this book to inspire young women to think about what it is they require, for themselves, to become happy and productive in this life. Preston's deep faith in God, personal belief in her ability to achieve her goals, and the desire to contribute something positive to the world is what gave her the willingness to start her own company and become a published author.

www.ingramcontent.com/pod-product-compliance
Lightning Source LLC
Chambersburg PA
CBHW061259040426
42444CB00010B/2422